on duty

D0028460

LIFE ON A SUBMARINE

Gregory Payan and Alexander Guelke

HIGH
interest
books

Children's Press
A Division of Grolier Publishing
New York / London / Hong Kong / Sydney
Danbury, Connecticut

Book Design: Nelson Sa
Contributing Editor: Mark Beyer
Photo Credits: Cover © Robert Garvey/Corbis; p. 5 © Yogi, Inc./Corbis; p. 7 ©
Navy News Photo Pentagon; pp. 9, 10, 13 © Photri-Microstock; pp. 15, 16,
18, 21 © Public Affairs Office/Naval Submarine School; pp. 23, 27, 29, 31 ©
Corbis; pp. 32, 35 © Yogi, Inc./Corbis; p. 37 © Roger Ressmeyer/Corbis; p.
41.© Corbis.

Visit Children's Press on the Internet at:
http://publishing.grolier.com

Library of Congress Cataloging-in-Publication Data

Payan, Gregory.
    Life on a submarine / by Gregory Payan and Alexander Guelke.
        p. cm. – (On duty)
    Includes bibliographical references and index.
    Summary: Provides information about the nuclear submarine, discussing
        the life of a submariner and the rigorous training involved.
    ISBN 0-516-23349-1 (lib. bdg.) – ISBN 0-516-23549-4 (pbk.)
    1. Submarines (Ships)—United States—Juvenile literature. 2. United States.
    Navy—Sea life—Juvenile literature. [1. Submarines.] I. Guelke, Alexander.
    II. Title. III. Series.

V858.P39 2000
359.9'33—dc21

                                                                    00-023358

CONTENTS

Introduction

A submarine is about the size of a football field, but only half as wide. It can house as many as 150 people at a time. A sub carries enough weapons to destroy any city in the world. A U.S. Navy nuclear submarine is one of the deadliest weapons known to humans.

Only three of every one hundred ships serving the Navy is a submarine. Only one of every one hundred sailors is a submariner. To become a submariner, a sailor must first meet very high academic and physical requirements. To serve on a submarine takes a special person.

A submarine can travel deep underwater or just below the surface.

The Navy Life

To join the U.S. Navy as an enlisted person, you must be between the ages of seventeen and thirty-four. Enlistment lasts from four to six years for regular active duty. Once you enlist and pass boot camp, you serve in the Navy for four years. Certain recruits must enlist for six years because they signed up for specialty training. This training includes nuclear operations, sonar, and electronics. Officers must enlist for six years.

After boot camp, a sailor may volunteer for submarine duty. This assignment requires further testing and training. Only men can serve on submarines. The main reason for this is lack of space. Submarines are small. They don't have enough room onboard to allow separate sleeping areas and toilets for women. Therefore, women may not serve on submarines.

Sailors are the backbone of the U.S. Navy.

BOOT CAMP

The only naval boot camp in the United States is the Great Lakes Naval Training Center in North Chicago, Illinois. Boot camp lasts from six to eight weeks. There, the Navy prepares a recruit for his or her years of service.

Recruits bring nothing to boot camp but the clothes on their backs. They receive everything they need during training.

On the first night of boot camp, recruits sleep in their clothes. The next morning they are sized for their military uniforms. Then their belongings are mailed back home in boxes. The Navy wants recruits to learn how to live their lives the Navy way.

Recruits wear sweat suits until their custom-fitted naval clothing arrives. During the first week, recruits also receive a shaved haircut and their official military identification tags.

Boot camp is a difficult experience for nearly all service members. Recruits are put

Recruits must be physically fit to make it through boot camp.

through a variety of tests. This is because serving on a U.S. ship is a great responsibility. The Navy requires all servicemen and -women to be intelligent and physically tough.

Boot camp is hard work!

Daily Life in Boot Camp

A typical day begins between three and four o'clock in the morning. Recruits must become used to performing their jobs with little or no sleep. This is because, during service onboard a ship, recruits often must do important tasks without much sleep.

Before daylight, recruits will have dressed, fixed their bunks, and exercised. Sit-ups, push-ups, running, and marching are exercises used in boot camp training. This training tests a recruit's toughness and ability to follow orders. By six or seven A.M., recruits shower and eat breakfast. More exercise follows breakfast and lunch. A five-mile afternoon run completes each day's physical training.

Boot camp also requires classroom training. The classes teach the history of the Navy, its fleet, and its role in world events.

Boot camp has many unusual tests which train recruits to follow orders and to trust their superiors. One test is the tear-gas test. Groups of recruits are given gas masks to wear. They are then led into a room that is sealed once they have entered. Tear gas is released. As the room fills, recruits are able to breathe wearing gas masks. They learn that their survival depends on the gas mask. When the room is completely filled, the recruits are told to remove their masks and breathe tear gas. Tear gas is a horrible irritant. However, it causes the body no lasting physical damage. The point of this drill is for recruits to learn to trust their equipment.

Each recruit's performance is reviewed at the end of every week. If a recruit's performance is judged unsatisfactory, he or she cannot continue boot camp. About half of the recruits fail boot camp. Sometimes recruits have to repeat a week of training. If that failed week is repeated successfully, a recruit can continue. Training is finished when recruits successfully complete all reviews. Then submariner recruits either can go home for two weeks or go directly to submariner school. Those not going to sub school will proceed either to duty on the surface fleet or to other training schools. If a recruit has enlisted in a submarine specialty-training category, he will learn that specialty before going on to sub school.

Nearly half of all recruits do not make it through boot camp.

Sub School

Recruits who hope to become submariners begin their training at Naval Submarine School in Groton, Connecticut. There, recruits are trained to perform duties on a nuclear-powered sub.

WEEDING OUT THE UNFIT

Sub school is similar to boot camp in some ways. The Navy continues to weed out people who may not be prepared to serve on a sub.

For the next eight weeks, recruits are subjected to a full schedule of military and technical subjects. Training courses are equally divided between seamanship, survival-at-sea techniques, damage control, and fire-fighting instruction. Students are given a basic course in submarine navigation, administration, communications, weapons, and maintenance.

Recruits must go through sub school before they become submariners.

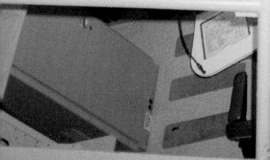

WARNING
DO NOT OPEN GATE WHILE
SYSTEM IS IN MOTION

LIFE ON A SUBMARINE

Anyone who does not pass sub school is assigned to the surface fleet. Students who have passed sub school but have not attended a technical training school enter service as a "striker." A striker determines what his specialty position will be after a certain amount of time served on the ship.

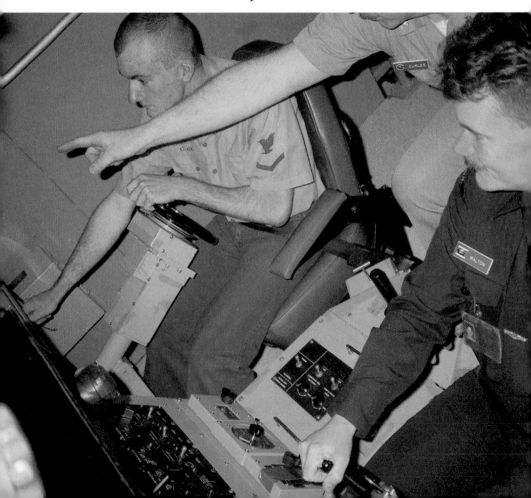

CLASSROOM TRAINING

Most of sub school training takes place in a classroom. This classroom training teaches recruits everything about a submarine. They learn how every working part operates on a sub. Because there is a limited amount of men onboard a sub, each recruit must be able to perform every task. When some crew members are off duty, the on-duty crew must help with whatever is needed.

SIMULATION TRAINING

Sub school has many different simulators that teach recruits how to perform well under pressure while on duty. These simulators are rooms that look and work exactly like the different parts of a submarine. Sub school teachers can stage fires, leaks, flooding, loss of electrical power, a broken pump, loss of nuclear power, or a computer that won't run. Recruits learn what to do during an emergency.

Submariner students learn how to perform under pressure.

FIRE TRAINER

The fire trainer teaches recruits proper fire-fighting procedure. An instructor runs the drill, controlling the size and location of the fire. He can run the exercise with or without lights. He can add smoke to the drill. He can stop proper air ventilation. Each drill requires recruits to properly deal with any emergency.

Wet Trainer

The wet trainer simulates leaks and flooding that might occur on a submarine. This drill takes place in a simulated engine room. Students must identify, locate, and control a leak. A leak can fill a classroom with water to the ceiling in a matter of minutes. Students leave the drill room carrying about twenty pounds of water in their clothes.

Escape Drill

The escape drill is designed to train a submariner to escape a disabled, submerged submarine.

19

A fire trainer teaches recruits how to fight fires on a submarine.

LIFE ON A SUBMARINE

Usually four recruits enter the room at one time. The room is flooded. Recruits are equipped with a Steinke hood to help them breathe underwater. The Steinke hood is a life jacket that has extra clean air a person can use for breathing underwater. Once the small room is completely flooded, recruits move backward about ten feet and escape through a hatch.

TRAINING SUCCESS

Recruits who complete sub school successfully are assigned to service on one of the most highly technical fighting ships in the world. Today's submariners will serve on either a ballistic submarine or a fast-attack submarine.

Crew members must know how to escape from a disabled submarine.

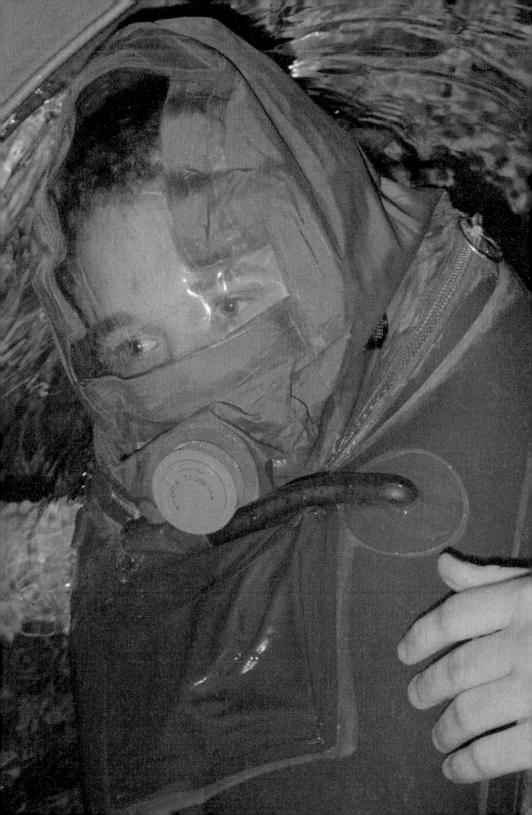

Submarines and Weapons

There are two types of submarines on which a submariner can serve: a fast-attack sub or a ballistic sub. Fast-attack submarines can perform many different missions. They can attack enemies at sea or on land. Ballistic submarines strike an enemy from under water. They hold nuclear missiles.

FAST-ATTACK SUBMARINES

Fast-attack submarines carry out missions that range from peacetime ocean patrols to wartime strikes against enemy targets. Crew members watch the waters off the shores of warring nations. They also gather information. Fast-attack subs are smaller than ballistic submarines. Living space is cramped. Crew members often share a bunk. When one person is

Submarines can fire missiles from under water.

sleeping, the other is on duty. Recreation and relaxation are done in the crew's mess (eating) area.

Weapons and Sensors

Fast-attack submarines use torpedoes, missiles, and mines to attack enemy ships and land targets. To find enemy targets and escape from enemy attackers, submarines use special electronic devices, such as sonar (see page 26).

The MK 48 ADCAP Torpedo

A torpedo is a long bomb that looks like a big fish. It has a motor that moves it through the water. It is used against both nuclear submarines and surface ships. The MK 48 ADCAP torpedoes are 19 feet long and weigh 3,695 pounds. They can strike targets more than 5 miles away. They can be used more than 1,200 feet under water. They travel more than 28 knots per hour (32.2 mph).

The Harpoon Missile

The Harpoon missile is a rocket that carries a bomb. It is launched from the torpedo tube inside the submarine. Once fired, it shoots out of the water and flies above the surface of the ocean to its target. The missile uses electronic signals to find the target. This is called radar (RAdio Detecting And Ranging). Harpoon missiles are 15 feet long. They weigh 1,400 pounds. They travel faster than the speed of sound (faster than 545 miles per hour).

What's a Knot?

A knot is a unit of measure. A knot measures the speed of something traveling on water. One knot is equal to 1.15 miles per hour. A ship traveling at 10 knots is moving at 11.5 miles per hour.

LIFE ON A SUBMARINE

The Tomahawk Cruise Missile

The Tomahawk cruise missile is used against targets on land. It flies very close to the ground at 550 miles per hour. It can fly distances of up to 1,000 miles. The U.S. military likes it because it does not need a pilot to direct it to its target.

Mines

A mine is a bomb that floats on or below the surface of the water. When a ship runs into a mine, the bomb explodes. This explosion puts a hole in the ship and causes it to sink. Mines are used near enemy harbors or where ships are known to travel.

Listening to the Enemy

Sonar is one of the most important electronic tools used on a submarine. Sonar transmits sound waves to find things under water. The sound waves bounce off any object in the distance, back to the submarine. Crew members

Submarines have bays from which Tomahawk cruise missiles are fired.

see these waves as images on video screens. It takes time for the waves to go out and return. The amount of time tells the crew how far away the object is from the sub.

BALLISTIC SUBMARINES

The job of ballistic submarines is to strike the enemy using nuclear missiles, if ordered by the president. Nuclear missiles are so large that the doors on each missile chamber weigh 8 tons (16,000 pounds) apiece. Experts say that one warhead can destroy a city the size of New York or Los Angeles.

These submarines' mission is to patrol the oceans. Crew members use sonar to listen for enemy submarines. They also wait for orders to fire their missiles. Luckily, such an order never has been given.

Patrols and Crew Life

A ballistic submarine patrols the ocean for forty-five to ninety days at a time. While on patrol, the sub stays underwater. When its patrol ends, an equal amount of time is spent in port.

A ballistic sub has two identical crews. They are called the blue crew and the gold crew. One crew will take the sub to sea for its normal patrol cycle. The other crew stays in port to train. Ballistic submarine crews are always

The U.S. Navy uses submarines to help patrol the oceans.

training. They must keep their submariner skills at the highest level.

After the sub returns to port, the new crew completes necessary repairs before the submarine goes out to sea again.

Life at sea

DRILLS AND TRAINING

During peacetime, there is a great deal of routine in a submariner's day. Regular drilling and training are a major part of a submariner's life. The idea is that, through repetition, response becomes automatic for when the real thing happens.

Chief petty officers (CPOs) use their experience to simulate things going wrong while out at sea. They can simulate any emergency at any time. Drills include fire drills, attack drills, and defense drills.

SUBMARINE OPERATIONS

There are many operations onboard a submarine when it is at sea. They establish what a submariner's day-to-day duties will be. A

Every crew member has important duties on a submarine.

submariner's duties fall into one of four departments: engineering, navigation, supply, and weapons.

Navigation

This department employs the quartermaster and electronic technicians. The quartermaster is in charge of Navy tradition. He knows which flags to fly while in port. He also knows the whistle system that announces when an important person is boarding or leaving a ship in

The weapons department makes sure everything is ready. . .just in case.

port. The electronic technicians steer the boat, read charts, operate the radar and sonar, and communicate with the base.

Weapons

This department takes care of everything dealing with a ship's weapons. A torpedo division is in charge of torpedoes. Fire control tracks targets. Sonar is in charge of listening.

Engineering

This department is in charge of powering the submarine and making sure that there is air for crew members to breathe. A submarine is powered by steam turbines that spin the shaft connected to the propeller. The steam is created by the nuclear reactor. The reactor is controlled by submariners who have completed nuclear training.

To make air for the submariners, water is sucked into the sub from the ocean. Its chemical makeup is broken down using a special machine. It separates oxygen from hydrogen in water. The oxygen is pumped through the submarine. The hydrogen is pumped back into the sea.

Supply

This department employs cooks, corpsmen, storekeepers, and yeomen. Cooks prepare all meals aboard submarines.

A corpsman is in charge of all medical needs. He is not a doctor. However, he can assist anyone who needs medical attention.

Storekeepers know where everything can be found on a submarine. There are thousands of lockers on a sub. Storekeepers can find whatever is needed, such as a spare part.

A yeoman is in charge of paperwork and record keeping. Onboard any naval ship, everything from requests for supplies to a submariner's performance review needs to be recorded on a form.

EARNING "DOLPHINS"

One of the most important events for a submariner is when he earns his "dolphins." This is a pin in the shape of a dolphin. Once earned, the pin is worn for the rest of a submariner's tour.

Dolphins are earned when a submariner's superiors have determined that he knows each of the boat's systems and how it works with all the other systems. A submariner often works for six months to a year to earn his dolphins.

Sleeping space is very tight aboard a submarine.

CREW LIFE

When a sub is at sea, a submariner works on six-hour shifts. There are three six-hour shifts in a normal day. The first shift is watch. Watch is doing whatever a submariner's normal duty is. The second shift is off duty. Off-duty shifts require submariners to do maintenance and cleaning. The third six-hour shift is set aside for sleeping. A submariner can sleep as long as there is nothing important that needs to be done.

Submariners take their meals at the beginning and end of each six-hour shift. The chefs onboard subs prepare great food!

LIFE ON A SUBMARINE

Close Quarters

Submarines don't have much space. Therefore, officers and enlisted men work closely together. On a sub, closeness is developed among submariners that is not often seen in other areas of the armed forces.

On ballistic submarines, enlisted men berth together in their own bunks in groups of nine. Beds are stacked atop each other in threes. Submariners store their personal belongings beneath their racks.

Fast-attack submarines have only three shower stalls for 130 men. There is only one clothes washer and dryer. The only place where a submariner can be alone is in his bed. Sometimes, submariners are forced to share a bed with another shipmate. This is called hot bunking. When one submariner comes off watch, the other goes on and takes the same bunk for the next six-hour shift. Officers berth together three to a room. The room is about the size of a walk-in closet.

Recreation

Movies provide the main recreation onboard submarines. Submarines have a good selection of both recent and classic films.

Reading also provides entertainment for submariners. Most subs have a librarian that keeps track of a small library. The library usually has enough titles to keep everyone happy.

Exercise is very difficult while onboard because space is tight. Most ballistic subs have some space for fitness equipment.

Crew members try to squeeze in some exercise when they are off duty.

Patrolling the Oceans

As you've seen, there is a set routine that everyone follows on a sub. Excitement comes when a submariner realizes he is on a ship that is an offensive weapon.

Military operations are usually top secret. These operations include navigating through enemy minefields or collecting information in hostile areas.

PORT

In port, a submariner's work continues. He is required to assist in maintenance work on the sub. A submarine has more than fifty miles of pipes and thousands of valves. The proper function of every piece of equipment is essential to the safety of the crew. There is greasing to be done and numerous filters to be replaced, all in the process of making the ship battle-ready.

Submariners do two types of maintenance while a submarine is in foreign and U.S. ports.

Some maintenance is done to prevent problems. Other maintenance is done to correct existing problems. Things can break on a submarine at sea and in port!

Shore Leave

Shore leave allows submarine crews to leave the ship while in the ports of friendly countries. Such places are called liberty ports. Most crew members are encouraged to leave the sub. Enlisted men are given thirty days' vacation per year. When submariners visit liberty ports, they get a chance to explore new cultures in foreign lands. In liberty ports they may sleep on the sub at night, but in general, they work one day and are off two to explore the area.

While in liberty ports, some crew members must always be onboard. They provide security and maintenance on the idle sub. Other times, the remaining crew relaxes or catches up on sleep. Everything is dependent on the condition of the sub.

Did you Know?

A corpsman gets his name from old foot-soldier units. These soldiers used to walk across the battlefield picking up fallen soldiers. Usually these soldiers were dead (corpses). If the soldier was alive, the foot soldier would help him off the battlefield and give him medical attention.

PROTECTING THE UNITED STATES AND THE FREE WORLD

A submarine is a powerful threat to any enemy. A surface target in a hostile area never can be sure if a submarine is just off the coastline, prepared to strike. Ballistic submarines have such great range that they are always considered within striking range. They are able to fire a missile from off the coast of North Carolina to destroy a target in Asia.

The U.S. Navy is proud to have its submarines fly the American flag!

Submariners often are isolated and separated from the rest of the world while on duty. It is possible that many submariners are away from family and friends for up to three hundred days in a single year. They rely on each other for support. They usually leave the Navy having made lifelong friends. They also have done a tremendous service for their country.

New Words

administration management of day-to-day duties

ballistic having to do with a missile that flies

berth a place on a sub where a submariner can sleep

communications sending radio messages

corpsman an enlisted person trained to give first aid and minor medical treatment

dolphins dolphin-shaped pins given to a submariner to show that he knows the sub well

drill (verb) to do something over and over, (noun) an exercise done to learn a skill

enlist sign up

fleet group of ships

foot soldier a soldier that is trained and armed to fight on foot

gas mask a mask that is used to protect the face and lungs from harmful gases

hot bunking when two submariners alternate sleeping in the same bunk

knot a unit of measure that measures the speed of something traveling on water

New Words

liberty ports the sea ports of friendly countries

maintenance work that keeps a ship and all its parts in good condition

mine a bomb that explodes when something hits it

missile a weapon thrown so that it can strike something far away

navigation steering the boat and determining its course

nuclear reactor a device used to control and release nuclear energy

patrol to observe for the purpose of maintaining security

port a place where ships can stay to rest and be repaired

quartermaster the submariner who is in charge of Navy tradition

radar (RAdio Detecting And Ranging) a device that uses radio waves to locate objects

recruit an enlisted member of the armed forces

seamanship the art of navigating a ship

simulate to imitate

New Words

sonar (SOund Navigation And Ranging) a device that uses sound waves sent underwater to locate objects

storekeeper the enlisted person who is in charge of supplies

striker an enlisted person in the Navy who has chosen his or her specialty

submariner a sailor who serves on a submarine

tear gas an irritating gas that temporarily blinds the eyes with tears

torpedo a cigar-shaped bomb shot out of a submarine

turbine a kind of engine that works using a current of fluid such as water, steam, or air

yeoman the submariner who is in charge of paperwork and record keeping

For Further Reading

Genat, Robert and Robin. *Modern US Navy Submarines.* Osceola, WI: Motorbooks International, 1997.

Hutton, Donald B. *Barron's Guide To Military Careers.* Hauppauge, NY: Barron's Educational Series, 1998.

Polar, Norman. *The Naval Institute Guide to the Ships and Aircrafts of the Naval Fleet.* 16th ed. Annapolis, MD: Naval Institute Press, 1997.

Sharpe, Richard. *Jane's Fighting Ships.* Alexandria, VA: Jane's Information Group, Inc., 1998.

Resources

The Navy Office of Information
Navy Office of Information – East
805 Third Avenue, 9th Floor
New York, NY 10022-7513
(212) 784-0131

Navy Office of Information – Midwest
55 East Monroe Street, Suite 1402
Chicago, IL 60603-5705
(312) 606-0360

Navy Office of Information – Southwest
1114 Commerce Street, Suite 811
Dallas, TX 75242
(214) 767-2553

Navy Office of Information – West
10880 Wilshire Boulevard, Suite 1220
Los Angeles, CA 90035
(310) 235-7481

Web Sites
Naval Technology – SSN Seawolf Class–Attack Submarine
www.naval-technology.com/index.html
This site contains information about different types of naval technology, including the SSN Seawolf Class.

USS Seawolf (SSN 575)
www.seawolf-ssn575.com
This site has information about the history of the Seawolf. It also includes links to other related sites.

Index

About the Author

Gregory Payan is a freelance writer living in Queens, New York. Alexander Guelke has been his friend for 15 years. Alex spent four years serving on the USS *Springfield*, out of Groton, Connecticut.